A Note to Parents and Teachers

DK READERS is a compelling program for beginning readers, designed in conjunction with leading literacy experts.

Beautiful illustrations and superb full-color photographs combine with engaging, easy-to-read stories to offer a fresh approach to each subject in the series. Each DK READER is guaranteed to capture a child's interest while developing his or her reading skills, general knowledge, and love of reading.

The five levels of DK READERS are aimed at different reading abilities, enabling you to choose the books that are exactly right for your child:

Pre-level 1 – Learning to read
Level 1 – Beginning to read
Level 2 – Beginning to read alone
Level 3 – Reading alone
Level 4 – Proficient readers

The "normal" age at which a child begins to read can be anywhere from three to eight years old, so these levels are only a general guideline.

No matter which level you select, you can be sure that you are helping your child learn to read, then read to learn!

LONDON, NEW YORK, MUNICH,
MELBOURNE, AND DELHI

Editor Kate Simkins
Designer Cathy Tincknell
Art Director Mark Richards
Publishing Manager Simon Beecroft
Category Publisher Alex Kirkham
Production Rochelle Talary
DTP Designer Lauren Egan

For Lucasfilm
Art Editor Iain R. Morris
Senior Editor Jonathan W. Rinzler
Continuity Supervisor Leland Chee

Reading Consultant
Linda B. Gambrell, Professor and
Director, Eugene T. Moore School of
Education, Clemson University.

First American Edition, 2005
Published in the United States by
DK Publishing, Inc.
375 Hudson Street
New York, New York 10014

05 06 07 08 10 9 8 7 6 5 4 3 2

Published in Great Britain by Dorling Kindersley Limited.

A catalog record for this book is available from
the Library of Congress

ISBN 0-7566-1163-6 (paperback)
ISBN 0-7566-1162-8 (hardback)

Color reproduction by Colourscan, Singapore
Printed and bound in China by L. Rex Printing Co. Ltd.

Discover more at
www.dk.com

www.starwars.com

Contents

STAR WARS™
GALACTIC CRISIS!

Written by Ryder Windham

PROFICIENT 4 READERS

Darth Sidious

Palpatine

Sith Lord
Although he appears to be a trusted Senator, Palpatine is really the evil Darth Sidious.

Secret identity

A long time ago, in a galaxy far, far away, a mighty Republic existed. All the different planets who were part of the Republic agreed to work together to bring about peace. Large armies were not allowed. Instead, the noble Jedi Knights were the Republic's peacekeepers. The Jedi got their power from the Force, an energy field generated by all living things. Their greatest enemies were the Sith Lords, who used the Force for evil.

One of the deadliest Sith Lords was Darth Sidious (SID-EE-US). This villain played a game. He was secretly a Sith, but he had another identity. He was also Senator Palpatine of the planet Naboo. Most people thought Palpatine was a kind man, but he was really a master politician who used people and events to achieve total power.

Palpatine was a member of the Galactic Senate, a place where Senators met to govern the Republic and discuss important matters.

Senate leader
Supreme Chancellor Valorum is leader of the Senate. He has to keep order in the Senate and deal with corrupt politicians from many worlds.

Government
The Galactic Senate meets on the planet Coruscant (CORE-RUS-SANT). Senators from all over the galaxy meet here to discuss new laws and other matters.

Young queen
Amidala was
elected Queen
of Naboo
when she was
just 14 years
old. She is
sometimes
known by
another
name, Padmé.

Naboo threatened

Both Palpatine and Valorum came from Naboo. Their world's government was a democratic kingdom, ruled by the elected leader, Queen Amidala.

Naboo's human population did not have an army, which made them easy to invade.

Palpatine wanted to gain more power. So he persuaded an aggressive trading organization called the Trade Federation to try to conquer Naboo.

The Trade Federation was run by aliens called Neimoidians (NY-MOY-DEE-ANS) who demanded that Amidala surrender, but she refused.

Valorum knew that some Senators would support the invasion because the Neimoidians had powerful friends in the Senate.

Valorum wanted to help Naboo without alerting the Neimoidians. He secretly sent two Jedi Knights, Qui-Gon Jinn (KWY-GON JIN) and his apprentice, Obi-Wan Kenobi (OH-BEE ONE KEN-OH-BEE), to the planet. Valorum hoped the Trade Federation would leave Naboo as soon as the Jedi Knights arrived.

Qui-Gon Jinn

Obi-Wan Kenobi

Escape to Tatooine

The Neimoidians were fearful of the Jedi Knights but were even more afraid of Darth Sidious, who told them to kill the Jedi. Fortunately, Qui-Gon and Obi-Wan evaded the Neimoidians and escaped into Naboo's swamps.

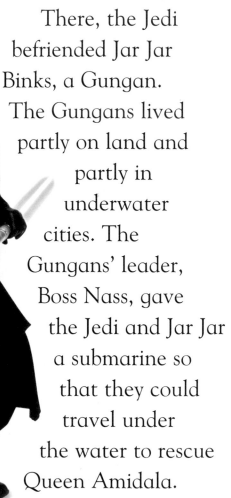

There, the Jedi befriended Jar Jar Binks, a Gungan. The Gungans lived partly on land and partly in underwater cities. The Gungans' leader, Boss Nass, gave the Jedi and Jar Jar a submarine so that they could travel under the water to rescue Queen Amidala.

Puppet leader
Neimoidian viceroy Nute Gunray appears to be in charge of the Trade Federation invasion, but he receives his orders from Darth Sidious.

Evil warrior
Darth Maul was trained by Darth Sidious. He uses a double-bladed lightsaber.

The Jedi and Amidala left Naboo in a starship to inform the Senate of the invasion. The ship was damaged on the way, however, and they had to land on the planet Tatooine (TAT-OO-EEN).

Meanwhile, Darth Sidious sent his deadly apprentice, Darth Maul, to track down Amidala's ship.

Gungan boss
Boss Nass is leader of the underwater city Otoh Gunga. He doesn't trust humans because he believes they think that Gungans are less important than humans.

Jedi friend
Bungling Jar Jar eventually becomes a representative of Naboo.

9

Criminal world

Tatooine was not governed by the Republic but was controlled by criminals and slave traders. While seeking a replacement engine for Amidala's starship, Qui-Gon and Amidala met two slaves: young Anakin Skywalker and his mother, Shmi, who were owned by an alien junk dealer. After seeing that Anakin was unusually strong with the Force, Qui-Gon helped him to gain his freedom and leave Tatooine.

Although Darth Maul tried to capture Amidala, the Jedi delivered her safely to Coruscant, where she told the Senate of the invasion.

Top criminal
Jabba the Hutt is the top criminal on the planet Tatooine.

When the Senate failed to take immediate action, Palpatine convinced Amidala that most of the Senate—including Valorum—was weak and useless. Palpatine urged Amidala to support a vote to replace Valorum with a new leader.

Friendly droids
R2-D2 is the starship-repair droid who helps Queen Amidala's ship escape from Naboo. He makes friends with C-3PO, a droid built by Anakin from old parts.

C-3PO

R2-D2

Power struggle
On Coruscant, Palpatine encourages Queen Amidala to question Valorum's leadership, then puts himself forward as a replacement leader.

An alliance
For her own safety, Queen Amidala disguises herself as a royal handmaiden. She finally reveals herself to gain the trust of Boss Nass.

Fight for freedom

While the Senate prepared to decide Valorum's future, Qui-Gon and Obi-Wan escorted Amidala back to Naboo. Although her people had long lived separately from the Gungans, Amidala asked for help from their leader, Boss Nass. He soon realized that Amidala did not think of herself as better than him and that the time had come to defend their shared world. So he agreed to help her to stop the Trade Federation destroying everything that the Naboo and Gungans had worked so hard to build.

Battle of Naboo
Brave Gungan warriors fight hand-to-hand with the Trade Federation's remote-controlled battle droids.

Meanwhile, Darth Maul arrived on Naboo with a mission to assassinate the Jedi and Queen Amidala. Qui-Gon and Obi-Wan were soon engaged in a furious lightsaber fight with the Sith Lord.

Jedi versus Sith
The Jedi fight Darth Maul on Naboo. Only Obi-Wan will survive the battle.

Anakin saves Naboo

Having traveled to Naboo with the Jedi, young Anakin tried to stay out of trouble but wound up piloting a Naboo starfighter straight into the Trade Federation's Droid Control Ship. He destroyed the ship, which caused the battle droids to suddenly stop fighting, and ended the invasion.

Obi-Wan defeated Darth Maul, but not before the Sith Lord had left Qui-Gon mortally wounded. Qui-Gon's final request was for Obi-Wan to instruct Anakin in the ways of the Force.

Winning strike
Anakin stops the Trade Federation's entire droid army by firing torpedoes into the Droid Control Ship.

As the Neimoidians were led away, Amidala learned that Palpatine had been elected as the new Supreme Chancellor. She had no idea that the invasion had been part of Palpatine's scheme to start a war in the Republic. Because she did not know, she and her friends happily celebrated what they believed to be their victory.

Yoda

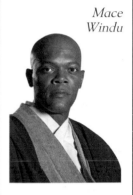
15

Lucky escape
Because
Amidala is
against a war,
she becomes
a target to
enemies who
hope to gain
from conflict.
An attack on
Amidala's
starship fails to
kill her because
she traveled in
disguise in
another ship.

Ten years later

Following the death of Darth Maul, Darth Sidious took a new apprentice, a traitorous Jedi Master called Count Dooku.

Ten years after the Battle of Naboo, Count Dooku led a group of planets who wanted to leave the Republic. These Separatists said that the Republic was corrupt and weak. This made it hard for the Jedi to keep order in the Republic, so the Senate considered creating an army.

Padmé Amidala continued to serve Naboo as a Senator when her term as queen had ended. She was against the building of an army. Shortly after Amidala arrived on Coruscant to vote against the creation of an army, an assassin destroyed her starship. Because the Separatists seemed to want a war with the Republic, Amidala suspected that Count Dooku was behind the attack.

Extended reign
Supreme Chancellor Palpatine secretly organizes a series of crises to stop elections from taking place. This means he can remain as leader longer than is usually allowed.

Double life
Count Dooku is secretly working with Darth Sidious. His other, evil identity is as Darth Tyranus, a Sith Lord.

Reunion
Padmé is glad
to see Anakin
again. But she
is surprised by
some of his
views that
are different
from her own.

True face
As she
lies dying,
the assassin
changes from
human form
into that of
an alien.

Padmé in danger

The Jedi Council asked Obi-Wan
Kenobi and Anakin Skywalker to
protect Senator Amidala. They
hoped to stop any further attempts
on her life. Anakin had grown into
a man in the years since Padmé had
last seen him, but, as a Jedi, he still
had much to learn from Obi-Wan.

After a second attempt on
Padmé's life, Obi-Wan caught
the would-be assassin, a female
hunter called Zam Wesell.
But before she could tell the Jedi
who had hired her,
she was killed by a toxic
dart fired by
a mysterious man.

The killer escaped using a jetpack. Only later would Obi-Wan discover that he was Jango Fett. Meanwhile, Padmé was still in danger.

Jango Fett

Clawdite killer
Zam Wesell looks like a human, but she is in fact a Clawdite. This alien species can change its form at will.

Armored man
Zam Wesell is killed by the man who hired her, a bounty hunter named Jango Fett. He makes his living by killing or capturing people for a reward.

Surprise at Kamino

After Obi-Wan and Anakin reported to the Jedi Council, Mace Windu instructed Anakin to take Padmé to the safety of Naboo. Meanwhile, Obi-Wan visited his old friend, Dexter Jettster, who was a weapons expert. Dexter identified the assassin's dart as a weapon from the planet Kamino.

Obi-Wan set off for Kamino, hoping to track down the armored bounty hunter. When he arrived, he was met by tall aliens who were expecting a Jedi to visit them.

The aliens, Kaminoans (KAM-IN-OH-ANZ), wanted to show Obi-Wan the army they had been building for the Republic—an army of clones. These clone soldiers were identical copies of a ferocious human bounty hunter.

The Kaminoans told Obi-Wan that a Jedi Master called Sifo-Dyas had asked them to build the clone army ten years earlier. This puzzled Obi-Wan because he'd never heard of the army. However, to gain their trust, he pretended to the Kaminoans that he knew about what they were doing.

Obi-Wan later discovered that Palpatine himself sent the mysterious Sifo-Dyas to Kamino to commission the vast clone army.

Clone makers
The Kaminoans are experts at producing clones.
They sometimes make money by creating clones for beings from other worlds.

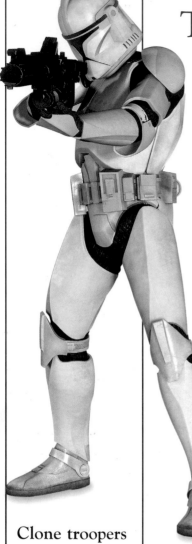

The clone army

The Kaminoan Prime Minister, Lama Su, showed Obi-Wan the enormous buildings where clone soldiers were made. They were born in special birth areas and trained to be obedient soldiers from a young age. The Kaminoans had already raised and trained 200,000 clone troopers and another million soldiers were nearly ready.

Obi-Wan soon learned that every clone was an exact copy of a bounty hunter named Jango Fett. The Jedi quickly asked to meet him. At Jango's apartment, Obi-Wan met the hunter and his clone "son," Boba. Jango said he didn't know the mysterious Jedi who ordered the army and said that a man named Tyranus had recruited him.

Clone troopers
Each clone is totally obedient and will follow orders without question. Despite their human appearance, the clones have few emotions.

Although Obi-Wan did not yet have solid evidence, he suspected that Jango Fett was responsible for the attempts to kill Senator Amidala.

Military exercises
When they are not sleeping or eating, the clone troopers train to perfect their fighting skills and be ready for combat.

Same son
Ten-year-old Boba Fett is an exact copy of Jango Fett. Unlike the other clones, he has not been altered to be obedient.

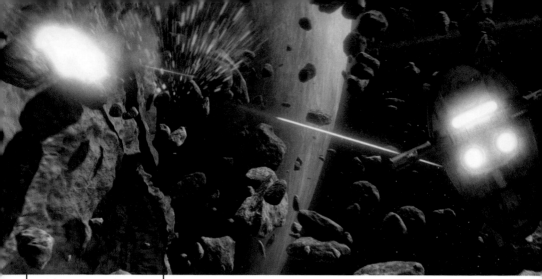

Space chase
Obi-Wan
chases Jango
Fett's ship
through a maze
of dangerous
rocks in space.
Jango fires at
Obi-Wan's
ship, but he
cannot shake
off the Jedi.

Secret plans

Obi-Wan told the Jedi Council about the clone army on Kamino. The Council instructed Obi-Wan to bring Jango Fett to Coruscant. Before he could, Obi-Wan was attacked by Jango, who then fled with Boba in their ship, *Slave I*.

Obi-Wan followed Jango. The bounty hunter's trail ended on the planet Geonosis (GEE-OH-NO-SIS). Millions of droid soldiers were being made there in a huge factory. Obi-Wan then spotted Count Dooku persuading alien business leaders to join the Separatists.

Tambor Watt, leader of the Techno Union.

Unified powers
Count Dooku wins over the greedy business organizations. He tells them that he will make it easy for them to trade anywhere in the galaxy.

Shu Mai, head of the Commerce Guild.

The Separatist movement was now renamed the Confederacy of Independent Systems and had its own army of droid soldiers.

Obi-Wan transmitted this information to Anakin but was captured by enemy droids. After Anakin received the information and sent it to the Jedi Council, he and Padmé raced to Geonosis to rescue Obi-Wan.

Weapons of war
The insectlike Geonosians make weapons. They build the droid soldiers for the Confederacy.

Count Dooku
tries to gain
Obi-Wan's
trust by
revealing
information
about the Sith.
He hopes that
by doing this,
he will learn
why Obi-Wan
is on Geonosis
and possibly
persuade
the Jedi Knight
to work
with him.

Taken prisoner

After he was captured on
Geonosis, Obi-Wan was taken to
a prison cell and trapped within
a force field. Count Dooku pretended
to be friendly when he visited the Jedi
and tried to convince him that
they didn't have to be enemies.

Dooku informed Obi-Wan that
the Senate was under the control
of a Sith Lord called Darth Sidious,
who had betrayed the Trade
Federation at the Battle of Naboo.

Dooku claimed he'd tried to tell the Jedi Council about the evil Darth Sidious, but they'd refused to listen. He invited Obi-Wan to join him so that they could work together to destroy the Sith.

Although Obi-Wan believed in the possibility of a Sith Lord in the Senate, he suspected Dooku was not telling the whole truth. Obi-Wan refused to join Dooku and remained a prisoner. After Anakin and Padmé arrived on Geonosis to rescue Obi-Wan, they were also captured.

No deal
Dooku promises to free Padmé and the Jedi if Naboo joins the Confederacy. Despite the threat of execution, Padmé refuses to surrender her world.

Execution arena

On Coruscant, the Jedi Council had informed the Senate of Obi-Wan's discovery of the clone army on Kamino and the Confederacy activity on Geonosis. The Senate would not approve the use of the clone army before a Confederacy attack. So Palpatine took advantage of Padmé's absence by tricking Naboo's other representative, Jar Jar Binks, into helping him.

Jar Jar proposed that the Senate should grant emergency powers to Palpatine. This meant that the Chancellor could deal with the Confederacy threat without having to wait for the Senate to vote.

Jar Jar tricked
Jar Jar Binks wants to save his friends on Geonosis. So he helps Palpatine gain the power to create an army for the Republic. Jar Jar doesn't realize he's been tricked by the Sith Lord.

No way out?
Padmé, Anakin, and Obi-Wan are to be killed by deadly beasts in the arena.

The Senate agreed and allowed Palpatine to activate the clone army.

Back on Geonosis, Obi-Wan, Padmé, and Anakin were sentenced to death in a giant execution arena. Suddenly 200 Jedi and thousands of clone troops rescued them.

Then, on the fields outside the arena, the mighty army of clone troops, led by the Jedi, went into battle with the Confederacy's droids.

Last resort
Although the Jedi prefer peaceful solutions to war, they lead the clone troops into battle on Geonosis.

In secret

As the Republic's army began to overwhelm the droids, the Archduke of Geonosis gave the designs for a super-weapon to Count Dooku. The Sith Lord then raced for his starship. Anakin was badly wounded attempting to stop and capture Count Dooku. He failed, and Dooku escaped.

Many Jedi died at the Battle of Geonosis. After the survivors returned to Coruscant, Anakin took Padmé back to Naboo.

Super-weapon
The Geonosians provide Count Dooku with designs for what will be the biggest super-weapon the galaxy has ever known— the Death Star.

The deceivers
The Dark Lords of the Sith, Darth Sidious and Count Dooku, never wanted the Confederacy to win the Battle of Geonosis. Their goal is to start a war in the hope that it will allow them to take total control of the Republic.

Hollow victory
Obi-Wan at first believes the Battle of Geonosis is a victory for the Republic. Yoda disagrees, as he knows the conflict is only the beginning of the Clone Wars.

Anakin's fellow Jedi had no idea that he and Padmé had fallen in love or that Dooku had also traveled to Coruscant to report to his master, Darth Sidious.

Secret wedding
On Naboo, Padmé and Anakin marry in a ceremony witnessed by R2-D2 and C-3PO. Marriage is forbidden for Jedi. So the event will remain a secret even to Anakin's friend, Obi-Wan.

Dooku betrayed

About three years after the Battle of Geonosis, the Clone Wars continued. The Confederacy's General Grievous abducted the Republic's leader, Supreme Chancellor Palpatine (who is secretly the Sith Lord, Darth Sidious).

Jedi killer
General Grievous is the Supreme Commander of the Confederacy's droid armies. Count Dooku trained the droid in the art of lightsaber combat. Grievous also takes orders from Darth Sidious.

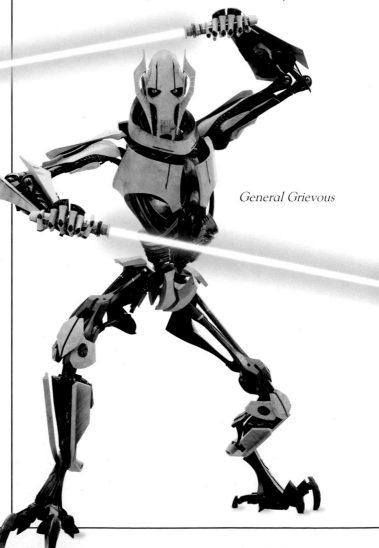

General Grievous

Obi-Wan and Anakin—helped by R2-D2—followed Grievous and got on board his flagship. Following a fight with Grievous, the Jedi found Palpatine held captive by Count Dooku. Dooku briefly overcame Obi-Wan but was brutally defeated by Anakin, who was urged on by the Chancellor. Dooku believed the Chancellor had a plan that would protect him. He was shocked when Palpatine ordered Anakin to execute him.

Although Grievous escaped into space, the Jedi successfully returned Palpatine to Coruscant.

Split loyalties

Shortly after Anakin's return to Coruscant, Padmé told him she was pregnant. Anakin believed this was happy news until a series of nightmares made him worry that Padmé might die.

Meanwhile, Padmé became more concerned about the future of the Republic. Chancellor Palpatine had made many changes to the laws of the Republic to deal with one crisis after another. These changes had increased his power and meant that he had remained Chancellor longer than was usually allowed.

Worried Senators
Padmé, Bail Organa, and Mon Mothma are among the Senators who realize that Palpatine is becoming a threat to democracy.

Padmé

Bail Organa

Mon Mothma

The Jedi Council was
also suspicious of Palpatine.
When the Chancellor made Anakin
his representative to the Council,
they agreed so that Anakin could spy
on Palpatine. Anakin hoped that he
would now become a Jedi Master and
was angry when the Council said
he was not ready.

Building trust
Palpatine
tells Anakin
important
information to
make him feel
like a friend.

**Caught in
the middle**
Anakin learns
that the Jedi
Council wants
him to spy on
Palpatine.
He feels torn
between his
loyalties to the
Chancellor and
to the Council.

Darth Vader

The Jedi Council learned that General Grievous had been seen on the planet Utapau. They sent Obi-Wan and two clone brigades to find him. Meanwhile, Palpatine revealed to Anakin that he was a Sith Lord. He made Anakin believe that only the dark side of the Force could keep Padmé free from harm.

After Obi-Wan defeated Grievous, Mace Windu and three other Jedi confronted Palpatine.

They demanded an end to
the Clone Wars. Anakin had now
convinced himself that the Jedi
had become his enemies. He decided
to turn to the evil dark side of
the Force and join Palpatine.
Together, he and Palpatine killed
the four Jedi Knights.

Palpatine made Anakin his
apprentice. He called the new Sith
Lord Darth Vader and instructed
him to kill the remaining Jedi on
Coruscant, then get rid of
the Confederacy leaders who were
hiding on the planet Mustafar.

Failed mission
Mace Windu
realizes that
Palpatine has
no intention of
ending the war.
He and three
other Jedi
attempt to
arrest Palpatine.
The Jedi do not
know that
the Sith Lord is
prepared to
kill them.

Total power

After Palpatine had gotten rid of his Jedi enemies on Coruscant, he ordered the clone commanders throughout the galaxy to turn on the Jedi Knights. As the clones had been trained to obey their supreme leader's orders without question, they did as they were told.

Surprise attack
The clone troops had always fought on the side of the Jedi. So the Jedi are totally unprepared when the clones open fire on them.

Yoda and the Wookiees
On the planet Kashyyyk, Yoda helps defend the Wookiees from an invasion of Confederacy droids. After an attempt on Yoda's life, the Wookiees Tarfful and Chewbacca help him escape.

Chewbacca

Many Jedi died, but Yoda and Obi-Wan managed to escape the assault and reunite with their ally, Senator Bail Organa of Alderaan. Returning to Coruscant, they learned that Palpatine was calling himself Emperor. He now had complete power of the Republic.

Soon, Yoda and Obi-Wan discovered that Palpatine was indeed the Dark Lord of the Sith and that Anakin was his apprentice, Darth Vader. They were determined to stop the murderous Sith Lords.

Evil Emperor
Chancellor Palpatine tells the Senate that the Jedi were responsible for an attempt on his life that left him scarred and deformed. No one dares to stop him from declaring himself Emperor.

Finding evidence
On Coruscant, Yoda and Obi-Wan view a recording that shows them Anakin has betrayed the Jedi and turned to the dark side.

Fiery planet
Mustafar is
a dark,
frightening
world covered
with volcanoes.
People live
on the sides
of great
mountains.

Attack on Mustafar

Searching for Anakin, Obi-Wan went to Padmé's apartment. Padmé was relieved to see that Obi-Wan had survived the attack but refused to believe his claim that Anakin had turned to evil. Anakin had told Padmé that he would be traveling to Mustafar to fight the Confederacy. But she told Obi-Wan that she didn't know where he was.

After Obi-Wan left, Padmé and C-3PO boarded her spaceship and set out for Mustafar, unaware that Obi-Wan had hidden in the ship.

End of the resistance
By having Anakin
kill the Confederacy
leaders, Palpatine
destroys the only
organized resistance
to his new Empire.

Obi-Wan hoped that Padmé might lead him to Anakin.

On Mustafar, Anakin carried out Palpatine's instructions and killed the Confederacy leaders. Moments after Palpatine learned of Anakin's deed, Yoda attacked the self-appointed Emperor. Despite Yoda's mastery of the Force, he was unable to destroy the Sith Lord.

Yoda versus the Emperor
Yoda and Palpatine battle with their lightsabers in the Senate.

Former friends
Obi-Wan knows that the real Anakin ceased to exist when he became Darth Vader. But it still upsets him to have to fight his own apprentice.

Terrible duel

Padmé arrived on Mustafar and confronted her husband, Anakin, about the terrible things he'd done. But Anakin claimed that his actions had brought peace to the Republic.

He said that he could use his powers to overthrow Palpatine and rule the galaxy. Padmé tried to make him understand that she still loved him despite his actions. However, when Anakin saw Obi-Wan come out of the Naboo ship, he became angry and choked Padmé with the Force. Though he didn't kill her, she collapsed.

Anakin and Obi-Wan lit up their lightsabers and began a fierce duel that continued through several levels of the volcanic world. After severely wounding Anakin, Obi-Wan left him for dead. Just as the Emperor arrived on Mustafar, Obi-Wan fled into space with Padmé.

Vader lives
Palpatine senses that Darth Vader is in danger. He travels to Mustafar on his Imperial shuttle to help him. Palpatine rushes Vader's body back to a medical center on Coruscant.

Helpful droids
R2-D2 and C-3PO bring the injured Padmé back to her ship.

Birth and death

Padmé was taken to the remote asteroid Polis Massa. There she gave birth to twins that she named Luke and Leia. Moments after their birth, Padmé died. It was quickly decided that the twins should be hidden, to keep them safe from the Sith. Bail Organa agreed to adopt Leia, and Obi-Wan promised to deliver Luke to Tatooine.

When Darth Vader awoke in a medical center on Coruscant, he found his damaged body repaired.

Jedi twins
Luke and Leia never knew their mother, but both will meet Darth Vader years later.

Suit of evil
Darth Vader's body is so damaged that he has to rely on an armored suit's life-support system to breathe.

He was now partly a robot and wore a suit of black armor. Soon, Vader recovered and was able to join his Master to begin work on the Death Star. He did not know that Padmé had given birth to his son and daughter.

More lies
The Emperor allows Vader to believe that he killed his beloved Padmé because Palpatine wants to destroy any trace of human feeling left in his apprentice.

The future

The Death Star would take many years to finish. The Emperor believed that every planet in the galaxy would fear the planet-shattering station and give in to his rule. Thinking himself all-powerful, he was not concerned with the location of the surviving Jedi.

Yoda traveled to Dagobah, an unpleasant swamp planet that was full of meat-eating life-forms. The small Jedi Master would remain on Dagobah for the rest of his life.

Death Star
When the immense battle station is finished, it will be able to destroy entire planets.